91 University Road

By May D. Kelman

to ALLACHBURN
with Thanks.
May D Kelman

New Generation **Publishing**

Hello, my name is May D Kelman and I was born in Dundee. I trained as a nurse at Bangour Village Hospital outside Edinburgh. Once qualified, I worked in Mount Sinai Hospital, New York. I worked as a nurse tutor in Leicester and also at the hospital in Malta.

I took a job as a nurse tutor in the hospital in Jamestown, St.Helena in 1997. St. Helena is a small island (10 x 5 miles) 1,200 miles from the nearest landmass in the South Atlantic Ocean. There is no commercial airport on the island and during my stay, the supplies boat arrived every 3 months, travelling from Cape Town. This presented me with a problem obtaining textbooks for my student nurses and, through my constant need for books, I had regular correspondence with a very helpful and witty gentleman, Brian Lewis at the bookshop at Queens University, Northern Ireland. I got to know Brian Lewis and his family well over the two years and, after I had left St.Helena in 1999, had the pleasure of visiting Brian and his family in Belfast.

One of the South African doctors I worked with saw some of my correspondence and immediately said: "Oh May, this is like the book 91 Charing Cross Road". When I asked for this book, I received by return a copy of Helena Hanff's famous book "84 Charing Cross Road".

So, here it is, my "91 University Road" showing correspondence, which started as orders for books but developed into a friendship and gives a snapshot of my life on St Helena.

On my return to Britain one of my jobs was as the manager of a care home in Aberdeen before I moved to Ballater. I am now retired and people who know me will also know I have Alzheimer's disease. Should anyone be interested in buying this book, I am giving all profits to Alzheimer Scotland.

I hope you enjoy this read of two very enjoyable years of my life!!

This is a journal of correspondence written in 1997 between May D
Kelman and Brian Lewis, the Bookshop at Queen's, Belfast.

Medical Department

St Helena

6/6/97

Bookshop at Queens
91 University Road
Belfast
BT7 1NL
Northern Ireland

Dear Ms Kelman

Colin Sullivan was with me yesterday, searching for the books, which you had requested. Wright, Tobin and Denham are all normally in stock but regretfully had sold out during last week at a seminar to local nursing home managers. However, Dr Sullivan picked up a couple of alternatives, which he will give to you when he arrives next week.

In the meantime, we are reordering your specific titles and we hope to deliver them to you on the August boat.

NICARE will be paying us for them.

Hope you have settled in. Please don't hesitate to contact me if you have further book requirements. We are in regular touch with David Bagley.

Very best wishes

Brian Lewis

M D KELMAN TELEFAX

8 Piccolo Hill
Longwood
St Helena Island

Tel/Fax + (290) 4756

Brian Lewis   Date 2 July 1997
Bookshop at Queens
Belfast
Northern Ireland

No. of Pages: 1

Fax   0 44 1232 666099

Message

Dear Brian

Many thanks for your fax of 6/6/97. I'm extremely grateful for the books you sent with Colin Sullivan. They are ideal. Along with the Care of the Elderly Course I'm now in the process of putting together a Counselling Skills Course for nursing staff which they feel is badly needed on the island. So once again I'm appealing to you for help!

Here is the list of books I require and hope you can send out on the boat in August. If you can't give the exact book I will be guided by you for the next best thing.

Developing the Practice of Counselling (1994) Dryden W   Sage Publ £8.95.

Introduction to Counselling (1993) McLeod J   Open University Press £12.99

Practical Approach to Counselling (1994) 3rd Edition Hough M Pitman Publ £13.99

Training Manual for Counselling and Helping Skills (1993) Nelson-Jones R
Cassel Publ. £15.99

I understand from Dr David Bagley that NICARE usually pay you then they deduct the amount from our salary. It saves us writing cheques and delays in the post if we miss the boat. I trust that will be OK for me too.

Do you have any up-to-date nursing catalogues for me to look through? I would appreciate any help you can give.

I look forward to hearing from you and, I am sure, ordering lots more books over the next two years.

Yours sincerely

May

May D Kelman

M D KELMAN TELEFAX

8 Piccolo Hill
Longwood
St Helena Island

Tel/Fax + (290) 4756

Brian Lewis
Bookshop at Queens
Belfast
Northern Ireland

Date 4 July 1997

No. of Pages: 1

Fax   0 44 1232 666099

Message

Dear Brian

Many thanks for fax of 2/7/97.

Please go ahead and send Burnard P (1992) 'Counselling' Buttterworth Heinemann Publ. along with the others.

Do you deal with any of the Open College Learning Materials or do I need to deal directly with them for their services?

I look forward to receiving the books in August.

Best wishes

May

May

URGENT

8 Piccolo Hill
Longwood
St Helena Island

Tel/Fax + (290) 4756

Brian Lewis   Date 17 July 1997
Bookshop at Queens
Belfast
Northern Ireland

No. of Pages: 1

Fax   0 44 1232 666099

Message

Dear Brian

I need your help again and time is getting short! I'm trying to change the nursing curriculum from a medical model to a more Project 2000 (as in the UK) one. My new intake of students arrive September 1st. Can you help? I was thinking along the lines of Sociology, Psychology, Anatomy and Physiology or Biological Sciences, Behavioural Sciences, Health Promotion etc. etc. All those that go along with the Common Foundation Programme for student nurses who are undertaking the Diploma Course.

Although the students here are undertaking a Certificate level of nursing education the curriculum is old fashioned and needs revamping and I'm trying to get it on the lines of what is going on in the UK. Do you get a book list from the University when the academic year begins? What do they recommend? Will be glad to go by what you suggest.

I'm in the middle of reorganising the nursing library which has sadly been neglected with books as old as 1960s which I feel are more dangerous than helpful. However not all are in that category and with a bit of imagination and forethought I might get the Course and the library on the right track. As Napoleon said, "the key to victory is to throw yourself in and see what happens." He should know, he lived here after all!

9

Look forward to hearing from you.

Best wishes

May

May

FAX

BOOKSHOP AT QUEENS
91 UNIVERSITY ROAD
BELFAST BT7 1NK
NORTHERN IRELAND
FAX 01232 666099

FROM BRIAN LEWIS: MEDICAL DEPT. ☎ 01232 666302, 666378, 662552

To   Ms M Kelman   17/7/97
         St Helena

Dear Ms Kelman

This morning's fax was the strangest coincidence. Adela, who works in our office, brought the fax to me at the precise moment that I was parcelling your counselling books for posting to Curnows Shipping.

As I suspected, Nelson-Jones is out of print, but I think that you should have enough material to be going on with. You might, at some stage, wish to take a special look at bereavement counselling. Only three publishers responded to my special request for catalogues – extremely disappointing!

PROJECT 2000 – All change this academic year as for the first time Queens University is responsible for nurse education throughout the Province. Upgraded members of lecturing staff have not yet been identified, therefore no reading lists as yet. Will send a note of some books which have been used in the past.

FAX

BOOKSHOP AT QUEENS
91 UNIVERSITY ROAD
BELFAST BT7 1NK
NORTHERN IRELAND
FAX 01232 666099

FROM BRIAN LEWIS: MEDICAL DEPT. ☎ 01232 666302, 666378, 662552

To   Ms M Kelman   18/7/97
        St Helena

Dear Ms Kelman

URGENT!

Project 2000

Were you hoping to receive
*   materials on the August boat?
#   Are you looking for books for use by student nurses OR
        resource material for yourself?
Single copies or multiples?
*   Parcels have to be with CURNOW by 30.7.97!!

                                                      Brian

M D KELMAN TELEFAX

8 Piccolo Hill
Longwood
St Helena Island

Tel/Fax + (290) 4756

Brian Lewis   Date 21 July 1997
Bookshop at Queens
Belfast
Northern Ireland

No. of Pages: 1

Fax   0 44 1232 666099

Message

Dear Brian

Many thanks for fax of 18/7/97. In answer to your questions,

1.   Could you please get the books if possible on the August boat.

2.   It would be resource material for myself, then I can order those
        that students would want in our library.   The pay here is
        appalling, they could not possibly afford to buy them. So any
        books I buy I will leave for their library. There are no book
        shops on the island, and the public library is limited and any
        decent books they do have are very old. OK if you like to
        collect old books but not for anything else.

3.   Single copies only for the time being. I'm happy to go by what
        has been used in the past as I'm sure they are better than what I
        have here.

Best wishes

May

May

FAX

BOOKSHOP AT QUEENS
91 UNIVERSITY ROAD
BELFAST BT7 1NK
NORTHERN IRELAND
FAX 01232 666099

FROM BRIAN LEWIS: MEDICAL DEPT. ☎ 01232 666302, 666378, 662552

To   Ms M Kelman   21/7/97

Dear Ms Kelman

In view of the urgency, there will be sufficient time for us to discuss the merits of various nursing books.

I am, therefore, frantically assembling four or five titles which I hope to post direct to Curnow's Cardiff office in tonight's mail, in the hope that they catch the August sailing.

I very much hope that they will prove acceptable and that you trust me to do this. Will fax a note of the titles within the next few hours.

Brian

Ross and Wilson A & P in Health and Illness I would have preferred to send TORTORA A&P but it won't be back into stock until next week – too late
Giddons Sociology
Atkinsons Introduction to Psychology
Naidoo Health Promotion
Taylor Sociology of Health and Social Care
Have included a free copy of this. New edition due November '97.

These should be with you 21.8.97.
Avoid like the plague books with the words "For Nurses." Or "....For Project 2000" as part of the title.
Use a good sound general textbook on the topic and then apply it to the nursing situation. I hope that they suit.

I am now completely knackered and I'm going home for a gin and tonic.

M D KELMAN TELEFAX

8 Piccolo Hill
Longwood
St Helena Island

Tel/Fax + (290) 4756

Brian Lewis   Date 26 July 1997
Bookshop at Queens
Belfast
Northern Ireland

No. of Pages: 1

Fax   0 44 1232 666099

Message

Dear Brian

Many thanks for putting together the nursing books for me and getting them in the post in time for the ship leaving Cardiff. I trust you implicitly in your choice of titles.

I now have one more impossible request to make, its every bookshop's nightmare! But take heart I don't need it now but would like it in time for Christmas which means being on the boat by 23 October 1997!!!! It's a book with every one of Shakespeare's quotations related to medicine. The book has been around for years. I saw it when a student nurse in the early 1970s and I know I saw it again this year, in fact I think it was in one of the Belfast bookshops when I was there in May visiting NICARE. Of course I don't know who the editors are or the publishers etc. so you do have a mammoth task/challenge in front of you. I'll keep my fingers crossed and hope you even know which one I mean.

I think you'll need more than a Gin and Tonic with this one.

Regards

May

May

BOOKSHOP AT QUEENS
91 UNIVERSITY ROAD
BELFAST BT7 1NK
NORTHERN IRELAND
FAX 01232 666099

FROM BRIAN LEWIS: MEDICAL DEPT.

St Helena

29.7.97

Dear Ms Kelman

Mea Culpa

I'm sorry

Brian

M D KELMAN TELEFAX

8 Piccolo Hill
Longwood
St Helena Island

30 July 1997

Dear Brian

Ego te absolvo!

If I hadn't opened my mouth David would never have guessed what was meant by the message "The quest for Shakespeare begins" (Lewis 1997) or words to that effect! So it was my own fault.

There are very few shops here so when it comes to Christmas presents it is very difficult to know what to get for people. David Murray claims to be a 'Sheakespearean Buff' and I thought he might like the book I have described to you.

I really appreciate your wit and help in my requests. I'll treat you to a G&T or two next time I'm in Belfast. Meanwhile please call me May. Ms M Kelman is terribly formal and I feel we are old friends now.

Regards

May

May

BOOKSHOP AT QUEENS
91 UNIVERSITY ROAD
BELFAST BT7 1NK
NORTHERN IRELAND
FAX 01232 666099

FROM BRIAN LEWIS: MEDICAL DEPT.

31.7.97

To Ms Kelman

Dear May

Many thanks for your absolution, which arrived here on the day that I carefully, reversed the Company Volvo into a parked car.

Shakespeare.

I haven't been able to identify a British publication such as you describe, but we are hoping to obtain Hill & Ottchen in time for Christmas. (it will be coming from Nashville – really!)

Best

Brian

ISBN	0-517-70446-3
Bowker Class:	INVECTIVE
	QUOTATIONS
	SHAKESPEARE, WILLIAM, 1564-1616 –
QUOTATIONS	
Author 1	Hill, Wayne F
Author 2	Ottchen, Cynthia J
Title	Shakespeare's Insults for Doctors
Physical	6in x 4 in; 80p. Trade Cloth
Publisher	Crown Pub Group: April 96
Price	US 12.50 dollars
Data Source	Bowker USA

BOOKSHOP AT QUEENS
91 UNIVERSITY ROAD
BELFAST BT7 1NK
NORTHERN IRELAND
FAX 01232 666099

3/8/97

FROM BRIAN LEWIS: MEDICAL DEPT.

SHAKESPEARE'S INSULTS FOR DOCTORS

I'm in stitches.

Brian

M D KELMAN TELEFAX

8 Piccolo Hill
Longwood
St Helena Island

Tel/Fax + (290) 4756

Brian Lewis   Date 9 August 1997
Bookshop at Queens
Belfast
Northern Ireland

No. of Pages: 1

Fax   0 44 1232 666099

Message

Dear Brian

Many thanks for fax of 31/07/97 and 03/08/97. I hope the damage to the Volvo and the parked car were small and not expensive.

Although the cover of "Shakespeare's Insult for Doctors" isn't recognisable, it looks good. I'm looking forward to reading it before I give it to David Murray. Don't be surprised if I ask for another copy.

Have given below another list of books for searching. I think they might be of use for the students. Could you give me a price so that I can hopefully order them for the library out of my education budget which is pretty poor. I've just ordered a very expensive Torso through NICARE so, have spent most of this year's money.

Regards

May

Roper Logan and Tierney (1990)   Elements of Nursing
Couchman & Dawson (1990)   Nursing and Health care
Research Scutari Press
McMurray   Community Health Nursing – Primary Health
Care in Practice

Gray & Pratt	Towards a Discipline of Nursing
Wright and Whittington	Quality Assurance An Open Learning Course
Burnard P and Chapman C M	Professional and Ethical Issues in Nursing Scutari Press
Thom pson, Melia and Bond	Nursing Ethics
British National Formula 1997py	
Trounce J R Clinical Pharmacology for Nurses? 13 Edition Churchill Livingstone	
MacKenna and Callender	Illustrated Physiology

I apologise that I cannot give publishers for all of the books. Hope you can help with some for the October ship.

May

M D KELMAN TELEFAX

8 Piccolo Hill
Longwood
St Helena Island

Tel/Fax + (290) 4756

Brian Lewis
Bookshop at Queens
Belfast
Northern Ireland

Date 10 August 1997

No. of Pages: 1

Fax   0 44 1232 666099

Message

Dear Brian

I forgot to add to yesterday's fax the following

2 copies – Bailliere's Midwives Dictionary (1951) ?7th Edition

8 copies – Bailliere's Nurses Dictionary ?22nd Edition

2 copies – Singer, A & Szarewski, A (1998) Cervical Smear Test. What every woman should know. MacDonald and Co.

Many thanks

May

May

BOOKSHOP AT QUEENS
91 UNIVERSITY ROAD
BELFAST BT7 1NK
NORTHERN IRELAND
FAX 01232 666099

11/8/97

FROM BRIAN LEWIS: MEDICAL DEPT.

Dear May

Things are now becoming hectic – University reading lists – hospital lists for pricing etc. This has meant that I have had time only to annotate your faxed list. Some publishers increase their prices in September of each year, so I suggest that you budget accordingly – say +7½%?

ISBN	0-09-181381-6	Availability : ip
Dewey Class	616.140754	Dewey Edition : 20
Old Class:	Medical Science	
New Class:	Medicine	
Author 1:	Szarewski, Anne	
Titlel:	Cervical Smear Test: A Woman's Guide to Testing Positive, Diagnosis And Treatment.	
Physical:	22cm. 0. 3r.e.of "Woman's Guide to the Cervical Smear Test" Paperback	
Publisher:	Vermilion: Aug 96 – *See Singer below*	
Price:	£7.99 (at 07/97) *x 2* = £15.98	

Roper Logan and Tierney	Elements of Nursing 4th ed 1996	22.00
Couchman & Dawson (1990)	Nursing and Health Care Research Scutari Press	13.00
McMurray 2nd ed 1993 Community	Health Nursing Primary Health Care in Practice	18.00
Gray & Pratt 1992	Towards a Discipline of Nursing	38.00
Wright & Whittington 1993	Quality Assurance An Open Learning Course	35.00
Burnard P and Chapman C M	Professional and Ethical Issues in Nursing Scutari	14.95
Thompson, Melia and Bond	Nursing Ethics 3rd ed. 1994	15.50
British National Formula 1997 copy No 33		14.95
Trounce JR	Clinical Pharmacology for Nurses 15th ed Churchill Livingstone 97	15.00
MacKenna and Callender	Illustrated Physiology 6th ed 1996	20.00
2 copies Bailliere's Midwives Dictionary (19920 8th edition £4.95 each		9.90
8 copies Bailliere's Nurses Dictionary ?22nd ed 1996 £4.95 each		39.60

24

2 copies Singer, A & Szarewski, A (1998) Cervical Smear Test What every Woman should know MacDonald and Co *If 1998 is correct then the book is not yet listed. See SZAREWSKI above*

£251.88

SAY   *£270.00*

M D KELMAN TELEFAX

8 Piccolo Hill
Longwood
St Helena Island

Date 11 August 1997

Dear Brian

Many thanks for getting back to me so quickly, especially at such a busy time. I forgot about Universities getting ready for the new academic year.

Please go ahead and order the books on the list when you have a moment. My apologies regarding the date re: Szarewski A. It should have been 1996. I had been busy all day (Yes! Even on Sunday) planning my teaching over the next two years so that I can decide when I can have a holiday. I was obviously concentrating on 1998, hence the date. We have to take our holidays after one year and all at once; but its difficult fitting six weeks in between classes and workshops and in-service training especially when you are the only nurse tutor.

I'm getting really excited as the boat arrives on 21 August with all the mail and my books etc. I never realised how much I would miss simple things as walking into a bookshop and browsing as I did for hours on end at home. Even Malta where I was working before coming to St Helena had a few bookshops where I spent many a happy hour. I also hope there is a lot of mail for me from friends and family. It is terribly expensive to phone from here and not everyone has a fax machine at home.

Must stop blathering and fax this to you.

Best wishes

May

BOOKSHOP AT QUEENS
91 UNIVERSITY ROAD
BELFAST BT7 1NK
NORTHERN IRELAND
FAX 01232 666099

26/8/97

FROM BRIAN LEWIS: MEDICAL DEPT.

Dear May

I hope by now you will have received the books sent on the August sailing.

I had taken a few days vacation at the end of last week, so I didn't see your fax dated 21st until yesterday.

Love to Jonathon the tortoise.

Brian

M D KELMAN TELEFAX

8 Piccolo Hill
Longwood
St Helena Island

Date 26th August 1997

Dear Brian

Christmas has come early to St Helena! The books arrived safe and sound. I keep picking them up and sniffing their newness like an addict.

Many thanks for the gift, it's much appreciated.

Although I've been on the island three months I still haven't seen Jonathon. Colin Sullivan, I think, managed to take a photograph of him when he was here in June. Last weekend Davis Murray and I visited Napoleon's house in Longwood. We had to get special permission and no guide. It was really interesting and the paintings were quite something but it would have been better had we had a tour and our questions answered.

I look forward to the October sail with more books and goodies aboard.

Best wishes

May

BOOKSHOP AT QUEENS
91 UNIVERSITY ROAD
BELFAST BT7 1NK
NORTHERN IRELAND
FAX 01232 666099

8/9/97

FROM BRIAN LEWIS: MEDICAL DEPT.

Dear May

Your library book order is now complete with the exception of WRIGHT: Quality Assurance, which is reported "out of Print".

All books will be with Curnow in time for Voyage No 37 – 23rd October.

Did you watch the coverage of Princess Diana's funeral? This was an event unique, I am sure, in everyone's experience.

Bye for now

Brian

M D KELMAN TELEFAX

8 Piccolo Hill
Longwood
St Helena Island

Date 9 October 1997

Dear Brian

It seems ages since we last communicated and I have another request. Although I am here for two years I still need to think of my future teaching career. As you are aware, jobs aren't easy to come by in the UK and I must show in my CV that I have been keeping up-to-date. I am thinking of undertaking a piece of research into "nurse occupational stress" as so many nurses here say they are stressed yet I find it hard to appreciate their kind of stress in comparison with their colleagues in the UK. I have been doing some reading around the subject but need a few articles and books dealing with this. I should be able to get articles through the Royal College of Nursing International Library but would appreciate if you could get me anything from the list given below.

Davis B D (Ed) (1983) Research into Nurse Education. Croom Helm London
Chermiss C (1980) Staff Burnout: Job Stress in the Human Services. Sage London
Payne R, Firth-Cozens J (Eds) (1987) Controlling Work Stress: Effective Resource and Management Strategies. Jossey-Bass San Francisco, California.

I'm in the middle of moving house as this one is about to loose its roof. I will be completing my move Saturday and will be staying at No 5 Piccolo Hill Tel/fax (290) 4616 thereafter.

I hope all is well. I'm looking forward to the boat's return when I shall have some more goodies arriving.

Best wishes

May

11/10/97

FROM BRIAN LEWIS: MEDICAL DEPT.

Dear May

Thanks for the fax handed to me yesterday.

Quiet autumn Saturday morning here – we have an Ella Fitzgerald tape turned low – "Everytime we say Goodbye ….."

Have started researches on your Stress Books. They look a bit elderly but I'll do my best. I'll also see if I can slot something a bit more recent for you.

Be in touch soon.

Brian

Best of luck with your move!

M D KELMAN TELEFAX

5 Piccolo Hill
Longwood
St Helena Island

30/10/1997

Dear Brian

Your faxes certainly make me smile, especially coming home after a hard day. They are very much appreciated.

Now for the next request. I'm sure you just wait for me to fax you with the impossible, but this is something different! Two requests actually!!!!

Request No 1 We are having a Burn's Night – 25 January. I need a Scottish poetry book or a Rabbie Burns one. After addressing the 'Haggis' a fellow Scot will address the lassies and yours truly will give the address to the ladies. But alas, all my Scottish poetry books are still in Aberdeen. Can you come to my rescue once more?

Request No 2 Every now and again there is a sale of CDs in the local market (if you can call it a market!) but 99.9% of the CDs are Country and Western. I would dearly love Mahler's Symphony No 9. I believe it's a double album. I've already got Mahler's Symphony No 7 and No 5.

I shall be forever indebted to you or I owe you three G&Ts now.

Best wishes

May

M D KELMAN TELEFAX

5 Piccolo Hill
Longwood
St Helena Island

05/11/1997

Dear Brian

Many thanks for the fax. You really are very kind going to all this trouble for me. Owen has faxed me Mahler so I have ordered the 1997 version, Cincinnati Orchestra led by Jesus Lopez Cobos.

My choice of poems are a follows:

Burns, R iii, iv, xxiii, xxvi, ciii, cxiv, cxx. I think that should be enough to give me something to work on meantime. I hope I have enough fax paper to take them, but the fax machine does have a memory so will store what it cannot print.

I'm sending you a few back numbers of the St Helena News and a photograph of where I stay. You can just make out the house on the right near where I live. I still have one film for developing which may have some interesting views which I will send on to you.

I'm off to a bonfire party tonight. There are no fireworks on the island so we can't have any disiplays. It's also my son's birthday and we always celebrated with a fireworks display. He is 18 years old today and now a young man. He's reading Computing at Robert Gordon's University, Aberdeen and loving it. I sent him a Birthday telegram. They still deliver telegrams from St Helena, which is rather different from the usual birthday card.

You Scots is nae sae bad either!

May

6/11/97

FROM BRIAN LEWIS: MEDICAL DEPT.

Dear May

It was fairly quiet this morning, so I was able to finish the photocopying.

I now have to do some cutting and pasting so the work should be 'ackshully' and 'toadly' completed by Monday or Tuesday.

I might have to send two or more transmissions to avoid awkward managerial inquisitions.

I was interested to hear about your son. I hope that he has settled into his (new?) regime.

I have a boy, Gareth who is a little younger – in the upper sixth at the moment. Gareth hopes to study medicine here at Queens but before then intends to gain a music teaching qualification as a 'safety net'. (Jazz, Piano, classical piano and church organ).

If you like slushy 1930s + 1940s stuff, we'll cobble together a cassette for inclusion in your next parcel.

There are now customers waiting to be served.

Bye

Brian

M D KELMAN TELEFAX

5 Piccolo Hill
Longwood
St Helena Island

08/11/1997

Dear Brian

I'm sitting in the back yard 'sunning myself'. The phone is in receiving mode, hence why you get my voice before I press the fax button.

Many, many thanks for faxes. I am now reading aloud to the cat and noisy birds. Glad you added "To a Haggis" – it wouldn't be a 'Burns Nicht' without that.

YES PLEASE to the cassette - with only 26 cassettes here with me, I've listened to them all by lunchtime – that includes "Teach yourself German".

There is a video "St Helena Island" and newspapers on the mail boat for you. Hope you get them in time for Christmas.

May

12/11/97

FROM BRIAN LEWIS: MEDICAL DEPT.

Dear May

What a strange coincidence!

"Teach yourself German" happens to be one of my all-time favourites. The bit that creases me utterly is when he says to her:

"Nach zweistundingem umherirren Kaman wir aus dej wald"

(After two hours wandering about lost, we came out of the forest)

And she says to him (sulkily):

Der holzfussboden finden wir nicht so praktisch wie den aus eisen"

(We do not find the wooden flooring as serviceable as the one made of tiles).

This stirring stuff and I eagerly await their next release.

Brian

5.50 ish

These pages were to have been faxed over the past couple of days. Now barely current. I'm hanging around because I have to attend a parents' meeting.

5 Piccolo Hill
Longwood
St Helena Island

12/11/1997

Dear Brian

You have a wicked sense of humour! You've made up that story in German, but it did make me laugh, and much appreciated.

I've just received the second lot of faxes as I was out running, approximately six miles. It's so hilly in places, wo you are reduced to walking up-hill and a slow jog when it's steep downhill. I sometimes run over the Half Tree Hollow where one of the doctors stays, then he brings me back in his car. It's difficult trying to find different places to run so I have to arrange for people to either drop me off and I run back home or I run to them and they drive me back. Our Hospital Charity Fun Run takes place 22 November, which I am organising as well as taking part. I'll be carrying a bucket, and hope people will put lots of money in it. The main part of the run is downhill so it should be relatively easy.

I'm looking forward to the books on "Stress" arriving. "The Managing Care" Series are usually quite good. I have one of their "Assertiveness" publications which I've used for teaching.

I hope you remember Gareth's photograph from the newspaper. He seems to be a very talented young man. I miss my son terribly, but I think all Mums hate having to let their sons go.

I'm listening to Mahler's Symphony No 1 'Tiatan'. I've just borrowed it from the doctor who gave me a lift home.

May

BOOKSHOP AT QUEENS
91 UNIVERSITY ROAD
BELFAST BT7 1NK
NORTHERN IRELAND
FAX 01232 666099

12/11/97

FROM BRIAN LEWIS: MEDICAL DEPT.

Dear May

I was surprised to hear that you had received your books as I was under the impression that the ship didn't arrive until the 21st. I had packed them myself and hope that they arrived in good condition.

Perhaps you could let me know when your own fax machine has been repaired. I have various bits and pieces to transmit to you.

B

St Helena School of Nursing
Public Health Dept.
Jamestown
St Helena
South Atlantic

Invoice date 12/11/97

Attention Ms Kelman

Curnow's Shipping Charges

Voyage 37   £20.00

To supplement our invoice No 03693

PUBLIC HEALTH DEPARTMENT
GOVERNMENT OF ST HELENA
ST HELENA ISLAND
SOUTH ATLANTIC OCEAN

TELEPHONE No. (2900 2520 FAX No. (290) 2530

From: May Kelman
        To: Brian Lewis

Dear Brian

Thanks for fax re: Curnow's Shipping Charge/

The boat is on its way to Cape Town and back to St Helena 21st November.

My fax should be working again now. The men repaired the broken cable yesterday. I left the phone in the fax mode this morning, so should be ready to receive!

Best wishes

May

5 Piccolo Hill
Longwood
St Helena Island

12/11/1997

Dear Brian

Many thanks for the faxes over the week. I did get the one that had your son's photograph printed on it. The fax page was stuck half way but no harm done. The fax/photo probably didn't do his justice, as it was a teeny bit fuzzy. I'm sure you must be very proud of him.

Your other faxes have me in stitches. They really are very much needed, as sometimes it can be quite disheartening here. One of the guys (who sometimes drives me to work) and I have a good moaning session every morning. This morning he came out with "Look on the bright side May, today might be the day the world will change!" It doesn't have the same effect writing it as someone saying it at 7.45 am (Unfortunately he leaves soon but with luck my own car might be fixed next week. I've been waiting six months for a gearbox. The saga is too long for me to write here and would bore you to tears.)

Dr Steven Isacowitz will probably be faxing you. (He is the third doctor here on a two year contract.) He wants some books, and as I am always telling him of your faxes and how you keep me in touch with reality he will be getting in touch. Do I hear a "not more work"?

I'm looking forward t o the Fun Run. Steven is going to film it using the new Camcorder!!!!

Best wishes

May

40

Thoughts while cutting my toenails

When to yon Half Tree Hollow you goes
Take advice from someone who knows
Breathe in not dust nor fungi
Nor especially, tungi
For they clog the wee hairs up your nose.

Maldivia House (time for a douse?)
Down the cowpath – St Andrews beyond
The Community Centre –
Got a job for a mentor?
Wirebirds can be seen near the Pond*

Ladder Hill? No, its too far away
That's enough to be sure, for today.
Back to Piccolo Hill or
You'll be ill – yes you will!
"Kicked Money Bucket" epitaph for poor May

- Topographical licence
- No Pond or Half Tree in the city
- No hollows at all. It's a pity

All the best for Saturday

From BOOKSHOP AT QUEENS

BOOKSHOP AT QUEENS
91 UNIVERSITY ROAD
BELFAST BT7 1NK
NORTHERN IRELAND
FAX 01232 666099

24/11/97

FROM BRIAN LEWIS: MEDICAL DEPT.

Dear May

This is to advise you that I have been granted Leave of Absence from 5.30 pm Friday 28/11/997 until Monday 8/12/97 in order to:

+ Finish re-decorating the back bedroom which I started din February (1996)

+ read Arthur C Clarke's "3001: Final Odyssey"

+ Build a Clootie Dumpling if I can find a clean pillow case.

If Dr Isacowitz wishes to contact me, perhaps we could work around those dates?

Hope that you're OK after the run.

Slainte whath, h-nite latha, no chi snach fhaie. Slainte!

Brian

M D KELMAN TELEFAX

5 Piccolo Hill
Longwood
St Helena Island

26/11/1997

MESSAGE

Dear Brian

Glad to hear the parcels arrived OK. The run went very well. I managed to collect in my bucket £120.50. My arms can now reach my ankles without bending over! The rest of the money has still to be handed in from the sponsor firms, but I think we will have done well.

My next ambition is to organise "The St Helena Challenge". There is a Malta Challenge and a Lazaroti Challenge that are marathons run over three days. What I would like to do is start the run at Longwood, into Jamestown as we did Saturday. BUT, then up the 699 steps to Ladder Hill, then follow the road back to Jamestown. It would be the only kind in the whole world and some challenge.

OK so you've got me this time! Last fax but one, (Monday's) the last sentence has me stuck. You win! I hope it is polite!

Steven did say he would contact you soon.

Cheers

May

May

M D KELMAN TELEFAX

5 Piccolo Hill
Longwood
St Helena Island

27/11/1997

MESSAGE

Dear Brian

Ok! So who has 'egg on their face'?

How about this, 'Go nein an bothàr leat Slàn!'

I got your message via the Education Centre at lunchtime. Thanks.

Enjoy your 'Absence of Leave' and hope you achieve all your objectives.

I'm off to a Thanksgiving Party at Steven's house. We have two American girls doing business auditing, so Steven has offered to have 'open house' for 50 people to celebrate. He will contact you when you return to work.

Slainte!

May

May

M D KELMAN TELEFAX

5 Piccolo Hill
Longwood
St Helena Island

7/12/1997

Dear Brian

Welcome Back! Hope you had an enjoyable break.

Do you know when Hanukkah is celebrated? Steven being the only Jew on the island doesn't celebrate Christmas so I thought he might like a Hanukkah present. I don't want to ask him as he will probably guess what I'm up to and there are no references I can look up here.

Thanks

May

P>S> You will need to give me more lessons re Irish Gaelic!!

6/12/97

FROM BRIAN LEWIS: MEDICAL DEPT.

Dear May

<u>This</u> morning's fax meant a lot to me.

Thank you.

<u>HANUKKAH</u> I fear that we are too late for this year, but perhaps you could prepare something for another appropriate time.

Brian

Possible problem on 4616 fax!

Recipes attached

M D KELMAN TELEFAX

5 Piccolo Hill
Longwood
St Helena Island

9/12/1997

Dear Brian

Have received all faxed. Number 3 and 4 very clear. I made the Almond Macaroons last night. Absolutely delicious!

You must be telepathic. I have Stephen and friends coming for dinner Thursday so I will serve the chopped herring as a hors d'oeuvre (only it will have to be mackerel as there is no herring) and the macaroons with the coffee.

Thanks. You're brilliant!

May

M D KELMAN TELEFAX

5 Piccolo Hill
Longwood
St Helena Island

9/12/1997

Dear Brian

I am just beginning to recover from your surprise call. It was really very generous of you and very much appreciated. Now that I can put a voice to the fax I welcome the faxes more than ever. However, I must apologise for my forgetfulness in not saying "over". I was just so excited to hear from you.

It must be quite a worrying time for you and your family with regard to your sister-in-law's operation. I hope all goes well for her and that she is able to enjoy Christmas.

It doesn't feel like Christmas here as it is very hot and sunny. Although there are a few decorations up in some of the shops. I miss the lights, and the snow, and the shopping, and everything else that goes with it.

The fax machine does play up quite a bit. I often put faxes through two or three times as I get a "communication error" following transmission. It is terribly annoying especially when I'm sending a fax abroad so I did appreciate all your attempts in the last fax. Thanks.

Goodnight

Yours aye

May

P.S. I'm actually Dundee born and bred. My husband was from Ellon, Aberdeenshire. We met in Leicester.

M D KELMAN TELEFAX

5 Piccolo Hill
Longwood
St Helena Island

11/12/1997

Dear Brian

The evening was a great success.

The herring ended up as smoked tuna and with a little bit of this and that was quite tasteful!

Steven enjoyed his almond macaroons.

The 'menorah' was arranged ad hoc but Steven recognised the shape as soon as he saw it.

So all in all its "Thanks" to you for all the frantic faxing and telephone call.

Thank you. It meant a lot to me too.

May

M D KELMAN TELEFAX

5 Piccolo Hill
Longwood
St Helena Island

16/12/1997

Dear Brian

Do you have any catalogues dealing with current novels/book of the month/yea etc.? As you know there are no bookshops on the island, and, although we all have our favourites with us it would be lovely to have available more choices. Can you help? The favourite doings its round at the moment is Bill Bryson's 'Small Islands'.

I'm working at home today as well as being a patient. I missed the radio message to boil the water following the latest heavy rainfall. I have been drinking the contaminated water – the rest you can guess.

Best wishes

May

PUBLIC HEALTH DEPARTMENT
GOVERNMENT OF ST HELENA
ST HELENA ISLAND
SOUTH ATLANTIC OCEAN

TELEPHONE No. (2900 2520 FAX No. (290) 2530

From: May Kelman   To: Brian Lewis

                                                           22 December 1997

Dear Brian

My fax machine tells me that I have a communication error again so I am sending this from work.

Steven says our relationship (you and I) reminds him of a film he saw many years ago. He thinks it was called "91 Charing Cross Road". It was about a man who owned a bookshop in Charing Cross Road and an American woman who wrote to each other for many years but never met. One day the American lady decides to have a holiday in London and visits the Bookshop. When she gets there the shop doesn't exist any more.

If I do visit Belfast when I come home for a holiday next June I promise I will come and say "Hello"! After all I owe you a few G&Ts.

Yours' aye

May

Mr Brian Lewis (Medical Department) BOOKSHOP at Queens

CHRISTMAS GREETINGS

Dear Brian

Many thanks for all the help you have given me over the past seven months, but most of all a big hug for bringing smiles and laughter from your witty and funny scripts. It is all very much appreciated when you are so far away from home.

Wishing you and your family a Very Merry Christmas and A Happy and Prosperous New Year.

Best wishes from St Helena Island
South Atlantic Ocean

May

BOOKSHOP AT QUEENS
91 UNIVERSITY ROAD
BELFAST BT7 1NK
NORTHERN IRELAND
FAX 01232 666099

22/12/97

FROM BRIAN LEWIS: MEDICAL DEPT.

Dear May

I went to our Admin building before 9 o'clock this a.m. and there was your greetings fax waiting to be lifted from the machine – a little "jerky" but perfectly legible. You rotter! You beat me to the draw. I had intended to compose an almost identical fax and send it tomorrow evening. However, this one can serve the same purpose. My wife, Margaret, my son and daughter, Gareth and Megan and of course myself wish you and your students a Happy and Peaceful Christmas and New Year.

May, I was on duty for the whole of Saturday and spent some time trying to photocopy the pages of Booksellers Buyers Guide in which you were interested. It isn't going to work. This means that I will have to include the whole catalogue with the bits and pieces that I have collected for the February Ship (Arrival about 12th March).

I find it very frustrating not being able to get stuff to you more quickly. You can tell Steven that I had weeks ago decided that you should have the Helena Hanff Omnibus which includes her famous 84 Charing Cross Road.

Christmas break: finish 4.30, 24th, off 25th and 26th. Plus 27th. Normal off duty. Back to work 29th.

Best

Brian

PUBLIC HEALTH DEPARTMENT
GOVERNMENT OF ST HELENA
ST HELENA ISLAND
SOUTH ATLANTIC OCEAN

TELEPHONE No. (2900 2520 FAX No. (290) 2530

From: May Kelman   To: Brian Lewis

                                                   24th December 1997

Dear Brian

Being a typical woman I have to have t he last word before signing off
for the holiday. Actually there is a change of plan. I will be working at
home all next week as PH Department is closed. In fact I am the only
person working here today. I'm preparing some lectures for January.
Next year will be very busy!

Steven and I laughed so much yesterday when we read your fax (to
him). It was absolutely brilliant. I hope you don't mind us sharing the
faxes but it is great to read them.

Steven is going to fax you today (be prepared for some Hebrew). You
will also be getting another pen-friend from St Helena. Gill Keay –
pest control, one of the avid readers (she's here on a 3-year contract –
has a PhD studying pests) is a super person. She too wants books.
Soon you will be writing to all the expats on the island. You shouldn't
be so witty!

Merry Christmas

May

From Isacowitz   Phone No. +290

24/12/97

To Brian Lewis

Dear Brian

From what I see of your faxes to May, you're a person of resources, from books to chopped herring recipes and the history of Chanukah. Not to mention your command of various languages that you write sometimes, none of which mean anything to me. But when you signed your letter to me 'Shalom' I decided to throw you a 'curved ball'.

On the subject of books, I recently re-discovered Philip Roth, and I'm now looking for anything by him. I read Portnoy's Complaint in 1970 (aged 15), and nothing since then (by Philip Roth that is) until now when I've become hooked. I've faxed you a list of his books, some (maybe all, I'm not sure) published by Vintage. I'd appreciate it if you could send me any books by him, but the ones I'd most like are 'The Facts', 'My Life as a Man', 'Deception' and 'The Counterlufe'. But I'd be pleased to get anything he has written. The ones I already have, and don't need a 2nd copy of are 'Portnoys Complaint' 'The Professor of Desire' and 'Sabbath's Theater'/

Please arrange for payment through Nicare in the same way you do for May.

Have a Merry Xmas and New Year.

Regards

Steven Isacowitz

M D KELMAN TELEFAX

5 Piccolo Hill
Longwood
St Helena Island

28/12/1997

Dear Brian

Hope you enjoyed your Christmas break There are probably a few faxes from St Helena waiting for your return. You are one very popular guy!

I am in the process of writing a long letter. I thought it might be nicer to have a letter rather than the usual demanding faxes. Then we can re-write 84 Charing Cross Road (to be names 91 University Road of course).

I am working at home until 2nd January 1998. The fax machine appears to be behaving so far if you want to fax me at home.

Best wishes

May

29/12/97

FROM BRIAN LEWIS: MEDICAL DEPT.

Dear May
!
I trust you had a good Christmas.   Being a typical man, I was
determined that you should not have the last word. On Christmas Eve
Gareth and I recorded two verses each from 'Adeste Fidelis' and 'Hark
the Herald Angels Sing' with the intention of playing them to you over
the telephone on Christmas Day. Unfortunately we were unable to get
through properly and your recorded message broke up and was
indistinct. I'll stick it on the end of one of your other tapes.

Hope that you enjoy your week swanning around at home.

I'm a bit concerned about the Hebrew. Will it be Biblical or Modern?

I might have to enlist the help of an acquaintance who is half Mormon
and half Jewish. His parents came from Salt Beef City.

Best

Brian

M D KELMAN TELEFAX

5 Piccolo Hill
Longwood
St Helena Island

29/12/1997

Dear Brian

The fax came through loud and clear. I was just on my way to Jamestown to do some shopping for the ingredients for the New Year party.

I really am very sorry that I didn't get to hear the tape put together by Gareth and yourself but I look forward to hearing it in March when the boat arrives. It was extremely difficult to ring out or to receive calls Christmas Day. I finally spoke to my son at 10.30 p.m. I had been trying since 10.00 a.m. He too was trying to call me but with no success.

I am very touched by your kindness in making the effort to contact me on Christmas Day. That means a lot to me.

Yours aye.

May

FROM BRIAN LEWIS: MEDICAL DEPT.

Dear Dr Isacowitz	MAY!	30/12/97
	HELP!	31/12/97

Overnight fax received safely.

I had already tried your home fax without success. Maybe the machine was not in the 'receive' mode?

You do not need to do anything about payment. NICARE receive an invoice from the Bookshop, pay the bill, then, I think, deduct the amount from your salary. I'm not sure if you are familiar with the British Book trade, but booksellers are given a (small) discount off a more or less fixed price. This means that we have to charge the carriage costs to St Helena – but only what it takes: Postage to Cornwall, then, later, Curnow's shipping charge to the island.

As I mentioned to May, I am frustrated about the length of time it takes to get back to you. When I helped refurbish the Medical Library at Port Stanley, after the Falklands conflict, the RAF would have flown my parcels to Ascension. I don't think that they would do the same now.

Biblical-Modern Hebrew to May. I must assure you that no political agenda was intended.

Brian

BOOKSHOP AT QUEENS
91 UNIVERSITY ROAD
BELFAST BT7 1NK
NORTHERN IRELAND
FAX 01232 666099

31/12/97

FROM BRIAN LEWIS: MEDICAL DEPT.

Dear May

Good Morning. No fancy Scottish greetings. I would just like to wish you 'Happy New Year' as I am off duty tomorrow. (Working Friday + until 12.30 Saturday). I hope that you all enjoy this evening and that all goes well. I am still having difficulty in getting a fax through to Steven. The calls are being accepted as phone calls, and I can hear people speaking, but the machine is not being switched to fax. Have also heard Steven's (?) recorded message. Is he South African?

Am looking forward to my letter. I hope it is enormous.

The next bit is for men only, so, put your fingers in your ears while you read this. Assuming that Steven was able to understand my Hebrew, I'm hoping that, as a qualified clinician, he can come up with a remedy for cold falafels. I realise that he might have to conduct extensive trials but look forward to seeing his results in due course.

Bye for now

Brian

M D KELMAN TELEFAX

5 Piccolo Hill
Longwood
St Helena Island

31/12/1997

Dear Brian

Tonight at midnight we will 'tak a right gude-wully waught' and wish you and Margeret, Megan and Gareth a very 'Happy New Year'

All the best for 1998.

Yours aye

May

THE END

On my return to Britain one of my jobs was as the manager of a care home in Aberdeen before I moved to Ballater. I am now retired and people who know me will also know I have Alzheimer's disease. Should you be interested in buying this book, I am giving all profits to Alzheimer Scotland.

I hope you have enjoyed this read of two very interesting years of my life!!

Life on St Helena was a wonderful experience but not one I would want to repeat.

As I considered my next experience, not knowing it would be contracting Alzheimer's, I wrote:

The Care Home was well presented
with speckless rooms and smiling faces.
It was the persuasion that I hated,
but the Home itself was well presented.
We sexagenarians should be invited
to consider, and voice, what we expected
of the Care Home which was well presented
with its speckless rooms and smiling faces.

Lightning Source UK Ltd.
Milton Keynes UK
UKOW050958120213

206156UK00002B/36/P